the joy of the morning

by Taryn Scarfone

JOY FILLED EATS

table of contents

notes on sweeteners

I use a blend of xylitol, erythritol, and stevia in my recipes. This is twice as sweet as sugar.

It is comparable to Trim Healthy Mama Gentle Sweet and Truvia.

joy filled eats sweetener blend

(twice as sweet as sugar):

INGREDIENTS:

- 1 1/2 cups plus 2 tablespoons erythritol
- 2 cups plus 2 tablespoons xylitol
- 2 tsp pure stevia

INSTRUCTIONS:

Process in the food processor for a few minutes if you are planning on using it in chocolates, beverages, or icing. For baking, you can just mix it together by hand.

alternative sweeteners:

- To sub in Swerve, use 1.5 to 2 times the amount of sweetener called for.

- To sub in Pyure or Trim Healthy Mama Super Sweet, use half the amount of sweetener called for.

Substitutions will work in most recipes.

Chapter One

make ahead for busy mornings

We all have those kinds of mornings where we barely have time to make a cup of coffee before needed to be out the door. These easy make-ahead recipes will save you from stopping for a carb-loaded pastry on your way to work. I have both savory and sweet options that are great cold or just need to go into the microwave for a few seconds.

almond crusted breakfast cheesecake

 20 MINS

 45 MINS

 1 HR 5 MINS

Cheesecake for breakfast? Yes! Packed with protein so you can eat it guilt free! My Almond Breakfast Cheesecake is low carb, keto, sugar-free, grain-free, gluten-free, THM S.

ingredients

CRUST INGREDIENTS:

- 2 cups whole almonds
- 2 tbsp sugar free sweetener
- 4 tbsp salted butter

FILLING INGREDIENTS:

- 16 oz full fat cottage cheese
- 8 oz cream cheese
- 6 eggs
- 3/4 cup sugar free sweetener
- 1/2 tsp almond extract
- 1/2 tsp vanilla extract

TOPPING WHEN SERVING:

- 1/4 cup frozen mixed berries per cheesecake thawed

directions

Preheat the oven to 350. In a large food processor pulse the almonds, 2 tbsp sweetener, and 4 tbsp butter until a coarse dough forms. Grease two twelve hole standard silicone muffin pans or line metal tins with paper or foil Ccake liners. I used a silicone muffin pan for this and the cheesecakes popped out really easily. Divide the dough between the 24 holes and press into the bottom to form a crust. Bake for 8 minutes.

Meanwhile, combine the cottage cheese and the cream cheese in the food processor (you don't need to wash the bowl). Pulse the cheeses until smooth. Add the sweetener and extracts. Mix until combined.

Add the eggs. Blend until smooth. You will need to scrape down the sides. Divide the batter between the muffin cups.

Bake for 30-40 minutes until the centers no longer jiggly when the pan is lightly shaken. Cool completely. Refrigerate for at least 2 hours before trying to remove them if you didn't use paper or foil liners. Serve with thawed frozen berries.

recipe notes

This makes 24 individual cheesecakes. They freeze really well! I wrapped them in plastic wrap and froze them individually. To serve just thaw in the fridge overnight and then top with some berries. I eat two for breakfast or one as a snack.

nutrition facts

Amount Per Serving: 1
Calories 152
Calories from Fat 108
Total Fat 12g (18%)
Saturated Fat 4g (20%)
Cholesterol 59mg (20%)
Sodium 131mg (5%)
Potassium 131mg (4%)
Total Carbohydrates 3g (1%)
Dietary Fiber 1g (4%)
Protein 6g (12%)
Vitamin A (5.4%)
Calcium (6.3%)
Iron (3.8%)

Nutritional Facts do not include berries.

low carb granola with almond coconut and sesame seeds

 5 MINS

 15 MINS

 20 MINS

This Low Carb Granola Recipe with Almond Coconut and Sesame Seeds has the perfect crunch with just enough sweetness to sweeten your morning. It is great by the handful or as a cold cereal with almond milk.

ingredients

- 5 cups unsweetened flaked coconut
- 3 cups sliced almonds
- 1/2 cup sesame seeds
- 1/2 cup sugar free sweetener
- 1/4 cup coconut oil
- 1/2 tsp vanilla

directions

Preheat oven to 350. Combine coconut and almonds on a large baking sheet. Bake for 5 minutes. Stir well. Bake for another 5 minutes. Stir and add the sesame seeds. Bake for 5 more minutes. Remove from the oven and stir.

Meanwhile, combine sweetener and coconut oil in a small pot. Heat over low heat until the sweetener melts. Add vanilla.

Pour the melted sweetener over the toasted coconut, almonds, and sesame seeds. Stir until coated. Cool. Store at room temperature in an airtight container.

recipe notes

Make sure to watch the nuts and coconut carefully while making this low carb granola recipe so you don't burn them. I can't even count the times I forget to set the timer and burn nuts while toasting them.

nutrition facts

Amount Per Serving: 0.5 C

Calories 343

Calories from Fat 288

Total Fat 32g (49%)

Saturated Fat 17g (85%)

Sodium 9mg (0%)

Potassium 315mg (9%)

Total Carbohydrates 11g (4%)

Dietary Fiber 7g (28%)

Protein 7g (14%)

Vitamin C (0.4%)

Calcium (11%)

Iron (12.6%)

chocolate peppermint breakfast cookies

 5 MINS

 12 MINS

 17 MINS

These are based on my Triple Chocolate Cookies but have extra collagen for even more protein and the zing of peppermint extract to wake you up. They are the ideal breakfast to grab as you are running out the door.

ingredients

- 3 tbsp coconut oil
- 3.5 oz bar of 85% dark chocolate chopped, divided
- 1 egg
- 1/3 cup sugar-free sweetener
- 3 tbsp cocoa powder
- 3 tbsp almond flour
- 2 tbsp coconut flour
- 1 tsp peppermint extract
- 1/2 tsp baking soda
- pinch of salt
- 1/2 cup collagen

directions

Preheat oven to 350. Line a cookie sheet with parchment paper.

In a microwaveable bowl combine the coconut oil and half of the chopped chocolate. Microwave in 30 seconds intervals, stirring after each, until it is completely melted.

Whisk in the sweetener and the egg. Add the peppermint extract, cocoa powder, almond flour, coconut flour, baking soda, and salt. Stir until smooth. Stir in the collagen. Fold in the remaining chocolate chunks.

Divide dough into six pieces and put on the parchment lined baking sheet. Press the cookies down a bit with your hand.

Bake for 12 minutes or until slightly firm to the touch.

nutrition facts

Amount Per Serving: 1
Calories 214
Total Fat 18g (27%)
Saturated Fat 11g (57%)
Cholesterol 31mg (10%)
Sodium 147mg (6%)
Potassium 172mg (5%)
Total Carbohydrate 10g (3%)
Dietary Fiber 5g (19%)
Sugars 2g
Protein 8g (15%)
Vitamin A (1%)
Vitamin C (0%)
Calcium (2%)
Iron (16%)

keto breakfast pockets

15 MINS

20 MINS

35 MINS

My Keto Breakfast Pockets will become your favorite grab-and-go breakfast! They are freezable so you can just pop one in the microwave before running out the door. You can easily customize them with your favorite breakfast meats and cheeses.

ingredients

DOUGH INGREDIENTS:

- 8 oz mozzarella cheese shredded or cubed
- 2 oz cream cheese
- 2/3 cup almond flour
- 1/3 cup coconut flour
- 1 egg
- 2 tsp baking powder
- 1 tsp salt

FILLING INGREDIENTS:

- 2 eggs scrambled
- 4 oz Canadian bacon or other cooked breakfast meat
- 1/2 cup shredded cheddar cheese or other cheese or your choice

directions

Preheat oven to 350.

Put mozzarella cheese and the cream cheese in a microwave-safe bowl. Microwave one minute. Stir. Microwave 30 seconds. Stir. At this point, all the cheese should be melted. Microwave 30 more seconds (it should look like cheese fondue at this point).

Put the melted cheese and the other dough ingredients into a food processor and pulse until a uniform dough forms. (Alternatively, you can mix by hand but make sure to knead the dough thoroughly).

Divide the dough into 8 pieces. Press each into a 6-inch circle on a piece of parchment paper on a baking sheet. It helps to wet your hands. Divide the filling between each circle of dough. Fold in the edges and crimp to seal. Place back on the parchment seam side down.

Bake for 20-25 minutes until golden brown.

recipe notes

These are freezable. Just cool completely, place in a plastic baggie, and freeze. Reheat in the microwave for about 1 1/2 minutes. Microwave times will vary.

nutrition facts

Amount Per Serving: 1
Calories 258
Calories from Fat 162
Total Fat 18g (28%)
Saturated Fat 8g (40%)
Cholesterol 106mg (35%)
Sodium 698mg (29%)
Potassium 236mg (7%)
Total Carbohydrates 6g (2%)
Dietary Fiber 2g (8%)
Protein 16g (32%)
Vitamin A (8.9%)
Calcium (28.4%)
Iron (6.5%)

sausage crusted egg muffins

15 MINS

40 MINS

55 MINS

These Sausage Crusted Egg Muffins are a great make-ahead breakfast idea for busy mornings. They reheat easily and are perfect to grab and go. Good mornings lead to great days. As a mom of four, it's important to me that my kids eat a nutritious breakfast in the mornings before school.

ingredients

- 1 lb sausage, casings removed
- 3 tbsp almond flour
- 3 tbsp coconut flour
- 3 tbsp ground golden flax
- 12 eggs
- 1/2 tsp salt
- 1/4 tsp pepper
- 1 cup cheddar cheese
- 1 tsp fresh rosemary finely chopped

directions

Preheat oven 400. Spray a 12 hole muffin tin liberally with cooking spray. Make sure to spray all the way up the sides and the top of the pan.

Combine the sausage with the almond flour, coconut flour, and ground flax. Divide into 12 pieces and press each piece into the bottom and up the sides of each muffin tin hole. Crack an egg into each. Sprinkle with the salt and pepper. Bake for 30 minutes.

Remove the tin from the oven and sprinkle the cheese and rosemary on top. Bake for an additional 5-10 minutes until the sausage is fully cooked (I stuck a meat thermometer into the crust to make sure it was 160) and the cheese is melted and bubbly.

recipe notes

OTHER FLAVOR IDEAS:

Caprese Sausage Muffins: Use sausage and proceed with the recipe as directed. When you remove the egg cups from the oven to add the cheese put a slice of fresh mozzarella on top of each. Bake for 5 minutes until it is slightly melted. Remove from the oven and top each with a slice of tomato and a sprig of fresh basil.

Spicy Sausage Muffins: Use sausage and proceed with the recipe as directed. When you remove the egg cups from the oven top each with shredded cheddar jack cheese. Bake an additional 5-10 minutes until the cheese is melted and bubbly. Put a slice of fresh avocado on each. Serve with spicy salsa and sour cream.

nutrition facts

Amount Per Serving: 2
Calories 246
Total Fat 19g (29%)
Saturated Fat 7g (35%)
Cholesterol 200mg (67%)
Sodium 462mg (19%)
Potassium 184mg (5%)
Total Carbohydrates 2g (1%)
Dietary Fiber 1g (4%)
Protein 14g (28%)
Vitamin A (7.2%)
Vitamin C (0.3%)
Calcium (10.6%)
Iron (8.4%)

warm chai pancake muffins

20 MINS

22 MINS

42 MINS

Warm Chai Pancake Muffins are a delicious make ahead and freezable breakfast! You can eat these cold or at room temperature but I prefer to microwave them for 20-30 seconds so the glaze melts and drips down the sides. It reminds me of pancake syrup on hot pancakes.

ingredients

BATTER INGREDIENTS:

- 4 eggs
- 1 cup cottage cheese 4% fat works best
- 4 oz cream cheese softened
- 1/4 cup almond flour
- 1/4 cup coconut flour
- 1/4 cup ground golden flax or additional almond flour
- 1 tsp vanilla
- 1/2 tsp cinnamon
- 1 tsp baking powder
- 1/3 cup sugar free sweetener
- 1 oz strong chai tea*

GLAZE INGREDIENTS:

- 2/3 cup sugar free sweetener
- 1 tbsp melted butter
- 1 oz strong chai tea*

directions

Preheat oven to 350. Put paper liners into 18 holes of 2 regular sized muffin tins and spray with cooking spray.

Put the cottage cheese in the food processor or blender and blend until smooth. Add the cream cheese and process until smooth. Add the other ingredients and pulse until they are thoroughly incorporated.

Divide the batter between the prepared muffin tins. Bake for 22-24 minutes until they are no longer jiggly and are golden brown around the edges. Let cool. The muffins will sink a little making an indent to hold the glaze.

To prepare the glaze stir together the ingredients. Divide the glaze between the cooled muffins. Store in the fridge.

recipe notes

*To brew the tea, simply combine 1 tea bag with 2 oz boiling water and steep for 5 minutes. You will use half in the batter and half in the glaze.

nutrition facts

Amount Per Serving: 1

Calories 88

Calories from Fat 63

Total Fat 7g (11%)

Saturated Fat 2g (10%)

Cholesterol 46mg (15%)

Sodium 82mg (3%)

Potassium 62mg (2%)

Total Carbohydrates 2g (1%)

Protein 4g (8%)

Vitamin A (3.5%)

Calcium (4.7%)

Iron (2.5%)

Chapter Two

savories

The perfect brunch menu has both savory and sweet options. Here are your choices of breakfast casseroles, quiches, and egg pies to please every palate. These serve a whole family but also keep well if you are only cooking for one or two. There are many mornings I heat up leftovers from one of my savory breakfast dishes as my breakfast.

broccoli & cheddar keto bread

5 MINS

30 MINS

35 MINS

This Broccoli & Cheddar Keto Bread Recipe is a great breakfast, lunch, side dish, or snack. It mixes up in 5 minutes and has only 5 ingredients plus salt. It is nut free, grain-free, gluten-free, and a THM S. It also reheats well on busy mornings.

ingredients

- 5 eggs beaten
- 1 cup shredded cheddar cheese
- 3/4 cup fresh raw broccoli florets chopped
- 3 1/2 tbsp coconut flour
- 2 tsp baking powder
- 1 tsp salt

directions

Preheat oven to 350. Spray a loaf pan with cooking spray.

Mix all the ingredients in a medium bowl. Pour into the loaf pan.

Bake for 30-35 minutes or until puffed and golden. Slice and serve.

recipe notes

To Reheat: Microwave or heat in a greased frying pan.

nutrition facts

Amount Per Serving: 1/6
Calories 90
Total Fat 6g (9%)
Saturated Fat 3g (15%)
Cholesterol 93mg (31%)
Sodium 342mg (14%)
Potassium 164mg (5%)
Total Carbohydrates 2g (1%)
Dietary Fiber 1g (4%)
Protein 6g (12%)
Vitamin A (5.5%)
Vitamin C (7.4%)
Calcium (14%)
Iron (3.6%)

loaded vegetable breakfast casserole

 10 MINS

 50 MINS

 60 MINS

This easy breakfast casserole is packed with colorful vegetables to brighten up your morning. It is my favorite way to get in veggies at breakfast time.

ingredients

- 1 tbsp avocado oil
- 1 red pepper, chopped
- 1 onion, chopped
- 8 oz mushrooms, sliced
- 2 cups baby spinach
- 10 eggs
- 8 oz cream cheese
- 1 tsp garlic salt
- 1 cup shredded cheddar cheese

directions

Preheat oven to 350.

Drizzle the avocado oil in the bottom of a 9x13 baking dish. Put the red pepper and onion into the baking dish. Bake for 15 minutes or until softened

Meanwhile, add the eggs, cream cheese, and garlic salt to a blender and blend until smooth.

Add the mushrooms and baby spinach to the softened peppers and onions. Pour the egg mixture over the top. Sprinkle on the cheddar cheese.

Bake for 35-40 min or until the center isn't jiggly and the edges are golden brown.

nutrition facts

Amount Per Serving: 1/8
Calories 294
Total Fat 23g (36%)
Saturated Fat 11g (55%)
Cholesterol 281mg (94%)
Sodium 430mg (18%)
Potassium 207mg (6%)
Total Carbohydrate 6g (2%)
Dietary Fiber 1g (5%)
Sugars 3g
Protein 15g (30%)
Vitamin A (37%)
Vitamin C (38%)
Calcium (19%)
Iron (9%)

cream cheese easy egg bake

 10 MINS

30 MINS

40 MINS

This is the ultimate easy egg bake or crustless quiche recipe. You make one egg mixture and choose your own veggies, meats, cheeses, and spices to go in it. It is low carb, keto, grain and gluten free, and THM S.

ingredients

EGG MIXTURE

(for one egg bake to serve 3-4 people, multiply as necessary):

- 4 eggs
- 4 oz cream cheese
- 1/3 cup half and half
- large pinch of salt

TOPPING OPTIONS:

- 1/2 tsp dill, basil, oregano, parsley, etc.
- 1/2 tsp dried onion and/or dried minced garlic
- 1/2-1 cup of shredded or crumbled cheese (cheddar, mozzarella, feta, etc.)
- sauteed veggies
- cooked meats

directions

Preheat oven to 350.

Put the egg mixture ingredients in a blender and blend until smooth.

Spray a baking dish with cooking spray. Put the topping in the baking dish: meat or vegetables on the bottom, then sprinkle on the cheese, finally sprinkle on seasonings.

Bake for 30 min or until the easy egg bake isn't jiggly and the edges are golden brown.

recipe notes

OTHER FLAVOR IDEAS:

Ham and Cheddar: Put about 1 C diced ham in the bottom of a sprayed baking dish. Sprinkle on 1/2-1 C shredded cheddar, 1 tsp driec minced onion, 1/4 tsp dried thyme, and 1/4 tsp dried minced garlic. Pour egg on top. Bake for 30 min or until the egg isn't jiggly and the edges are golden brown.

Broccoli and Cheese: Cut 1 head of broccoli into small pieces. Steam in the microwave or a saucepan until tender. Put in the bottom of a baking dish sprayed with cooking spray. Sprinkle 1/2-1 C shredded cheese on top. Pour egg on top. Bake for 30 min or until the egg isn't jiggly and the edges are golden brown.

nutrition facts

Amount Per Serving: 1

Calories 243

Calories from Fat 180

Total Fat 20g (31%)

Saturated Fat 11g (55%)

Cholesterol 217mg (72%)

Sodium 249mg (10%)

Potassium 139mg (4%)

Total Carbohydrates 2g (1%)

Protein 11g (22%)

Vitamin A (16.6%)

Calcium (17.5%)

Iron (5.4%)

breakfast egg & sausage pie

 5 MINS

 1 HR

 1 HR 5 MINS

This Breakfast Egg & Sausage Pie only takes a few minutes to prepare. With just 5 ingredients it is the ultimate easy family friendly breakfast.

ingredients

- 1 lb sausage
- 2 tbsp coconut flour
- 10 eggs
- 1 tsp garlic salt
- 1 cup shredded cheese

directions

Preheat oven to 350.

Spray a deep dish glass pie plate with cooking spray. Mix together the sausage and coconut flour in the pie plate and then press it out along the bottom and up the sides.

Crack the eggs into the pie plate on top of the sausage. Sprinkle with the garlic salt.

Bake for 45 minutes. Sprinkle with the cheese. Bake for an additional 15 minutes or until the eggs have set and the cheese is melted.

nutrition facts

Amount Per Serving: 1/8
Calories 300
Calories from Fat 207
Total Fat 23g (35%)
Saturated Fat 23g (40%)
Cholesterol 256mg (85%)
Sodium 820mg (34%)
Potassium 227mg (6%)
Total Carbohydrates 1g (0%)
Protein 18g (36%)
Vitamin A (78.7%)
Vitamin C (0.5%)
Calcium (10.7%)
Iron (9.4%)

asparagus quiche

 5 MINS

 45 MINS

 50 MINS

With only 3 ingredients this asparagus quiche is the ideal easy brunch entree.

ingredients

ROAST ASPARAGUS:

- 1 tbsp butter flavored coconut oil
- 2 lb asparagus trimmed to remove the tough ends

CRUSTLESS QUICHE:

- 10 eggs
- 2 tbsp butter flavored coconut oil
- 1 tsp salt

directions

Preheat oven to 425.

Put 1 Tbsp of coconut oil on a large rimmed baking sheet. Add the asparagus. Roast the asparagus for 15 minutes or until crisp tender.

Meanwhile, combine the eggs, 2 Tbsps coconut oil and salt in a blender. Process until smooth.

Reduce the oven to 350. Put the roast asparagus in a large greased quiche pan or casserole dish. Pour the egg mixture over the asparagus.

Bake for 30 minutes or until the egg has set in the center and no longer jiggles.

recipe notes

I always encourage my readers to tweak recipes to their tastes. Love bacon? Go ahead and add some. Don't care about this being dairy-free? Toss in some cheese. I'd love to try it with a herbed goat cheese. Have an abundance of fresh herbs in your garden? Chop up with basil and sprinkle it in. I thought about adding some sun-dried tomatoes but decided that 3 was the magic number for this recipe.

nutrition facts

Amount Per Serving: 1/8

Calories 145

Calories from Fat 90

Total Fat 10g (15%)

Saturated Fat 6g (30%)

Cholesterol 204mg (68%)

Sodium 371mg (15%)

Potassium 304mg (9%)

Total Carbohydrates 4g (1%)

Dietary Fiber 2g (8%)

Protein 9g (18%)

Vitamin A (23.1%)

Vitamin C (7.7%)

Calcium (5.8%)

Iron (18.8%)

ricotta & sausage breakfast casserole

 10 MINS

 55 MINS

 1 HR 5 MINS

My Ricotta & Sausage Breakfast Casserole is very easy to put together with 6 ingredients but impressive enough to wow your family and friends. With fresh tomatoes, basil, ricotta cheese, and sausage it is flavorful and delicious.

ingredients

- 2 - 2.5 pounds Italian sausage
- 10 eggs
- 4 oz cream cheese
- 16 oz ricotta
- 12 cherry tomatoes
- 1 tbsp chopped basil
- 1 tsp salt divided

directions

Preheat oven to 400.

Put sausage in the bottom of a large casserole dish. Bake for 20 minutes. Remove from the oven and carefully drain. I drained over a C of oil and cooking liquid. Break the sausage up into small pieces using a potato masher.

Blend the eggs and cream cheese until smooth. Pour over the cooked, drained sausage. Sprinkle with 1/2 tsp salt. Put blobs of ricotta on top. Distribute the tomatoes evenly. Sprinkle with the chopped basil and remaining 1/2 tsp salt.

Bake for an additional 35-40 minutes until the eggs have set.

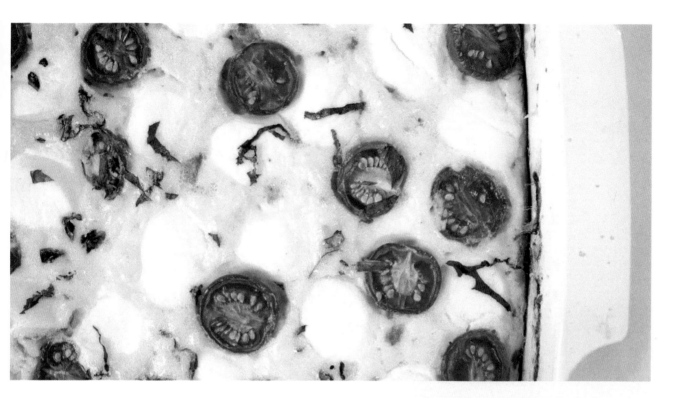

recipe notes

I used a small one tablespoon cookie scoop to drop the balls of ricotta on top of the casserole. You could use a teaspoon if you don't have a cookie scoop but I recommend getting one. That is one of my favorite kitchen gadgets. I have three different sizes and use them all frequently.

nutrition facts

Amount Per Serving: 1/12
Calories 415
Calories from Fat 315
Total Fat 35g (54%)
Saturated Fat 14g (70%)
Cholesterol 223mg (74%)
Sodium 862mg (36%)
Potassium 331mg (9%)
Total Carbohydrates 2g (1%)
Protein 20g (40%)
Vitamin A (11.5%)
Vitamin C (6.5%)
Calcium (12.4%)
Iron (10.2%)

Chapter Three

pancakes & waffles

Pancakes and waffles can be missed when you switch to a low carb or keto diet. I'm here to make sure that doesn't happen. These recipes mix up in just a few minutes and satisfy your sweet breakfast craving. From Classic Vanilla Waffles to Pumpkin Rolls Pancakes your mornings will be more joyful with every sweet bite.

easy flourless almond low carb waffles

5 MINS

5 MINS

10 MINS

These Easy Flourless Almond Low Carb Waffles make it into your waffle iron after only a 5-minute prep. Just give the ingredients a whirl in the blender and you are good to go! They are moist, flavorful, and freeze and reheat well!

ingredients

- 2 cups blanched slivered almonds
- 1/4 cup sugar free sweetener
- 1/2 cup cottage cheese
- 1/2 cup almond milk
- 4 eggs
- 1 tsp baking powder
- 1 tsp almond extract

directions

Preheat your waffle iron according to manufacturer's instructions.

Put the almonds and sweetener in the blender and blend until finely ground. Add the other ingredients and blend until smooth.

Spray the waffle iron with cooking spray. Pour about 1/4 of the batter into the waffle iron. If you have a smaller waffle iron you will use less batter. Just pour enough to cover 3/4 of the bottom grill. Cook until golden brown.

To make crisper waffles let the waffles cool and then toast in the toaster.

recipe notes

These waffles freeze well! Make a big batch, freeze some, and then just pop them in the toaster whenever you want one.

They are so filling that sometimes I'll just eat 1/2 of a waffle with some yogurt and berries or on the side with eggs and bacon.

nutrition facts

Amount Per Serving: 1

Calories 415

Calories from Fat 306

Total Fat 34g (52%)

Saturated Fat 3g (15%)

Cholesterol 168mg (56%)

Sodium 210mg (9%)

Potassium 570mg (16%)

Total Carbohydrates 12g (4%)

Dietary Fiber 5g (20%)

Protein 20g (40%)

Vitamin A (5.5%)

Calcium (26.6%)

Iron (14.7%)

cinnamon roll waffles with cream cheese icing

10 MINS

10 MINS

20 MINS

My Cinnamon Roll Waffles with Cream Cheese Icing will satisfy all your cravings. They are rich & filling with sweet cinnamon & creamy icing.

ingredients

WAFFLE BATTER:

- 4 eggs
- 1 cup cottage cheese 4% works best
- 4 oz cream cheese softened
- 1/3 cup almond flour
- 1/3 cup coconut flour
- 1/3 cup ground golden flax or additional almond flour
- 1 tsp vanilla
- 1 tsp baking powder or soda
- 1/3 cup sugar free sweetener

CINNAMON SWIRL:

- 2 tbsp melted butter
- 2 tbsp sugar free sweetener
- 2 tbsp cinnamon

ICING:

- 4 oz cream cheese softened
- 1/4 C sugar free sweetener

directions

Put the cottage cheese in the food processor and blend until smooth. Add the cream cheese and process until smooth. Add the other ingredients and pulse until they are thoroughly incorporated.

Stir together the ingredients for the cinnamon swirl.

Spray your waffle iron with cooking spray. Spoon on the batter and drizzle on some of the cinnamon swirl. Swirl it in gently with a toothpick, knife, or spoon. (I put it in a ziploc and piped a swirl but you really couldn't see it after it was cooked so don't bother).

Cook until golden brown. Remove carefully. Repeat until all the batter is used up.

While the waffles are cooking stir together icing ingredients and set aside. Divide the icing between the waffles and serve.

nutrition facts

Amount Per Serving: 1
Calories 530
Calories from Fat 405
Total Fat 45g (69%)
Saturated Fat 17g (85%)
Cholesterol 250mg (83%)
Sodium 486mg (20%)
Potassium 210mg (6%)
Total Carbohydrates 13g (4%)
Dietary Fiber 5g (20%)
Protein 20g (40%)
Vitamin A (25%)
Calcium (22.2%)
Iron (13.2%)

classic vanilla waffles with almond flour

 5 MINS

 10 MINS

 15 MINS

These Classic Vanilla Waffles with Almond Flour are my favorite weekend breakfast. With a dollop of jam and some fresh berries, they beat any other waffle hands down.

ingredients

- 6 eggs
- 1 cup 2% or 4% milkfat cottage cheese
- 4 oz cream cheese softened
- 1 cup almond flour
- 1/2 cup coconut flour
- 1/3 cup sugar free sweetener
- 2 tsp vanilla
- 1 tsp baking powder

directions

Preheat a waffle iron.

Add all the ingredients to a blender. Blend until smooth, scraping down the sides as necessary.

Grease the waffle iron. Pour about 3/4 C of batter onto the waffle iron (less if you are not using a Belgian waffle iron).

Cook until deep golden brown. Your waffle iron's ready light may turn on before this happens. Just ignore it. Gently loosen and remove the waffle.

Repeat with the remaining batter.

recipe notes

You can sub Trim Healthy Mama Baking Blend for the almond and coconut flours in this recipe.

nutrition facts

Amount Per Serving: 1
Calories 314
Calories from Fat 198
Total Fat 22g (34%)
Saturated Fat 7g (35%)
Cholesterol 190mg (63%)
Sodium 272mg (11%)
Potassium 207mg (6%)
Total Carbohydrates 12g (4%)
Dietary Fiber 5g (20%)
Protein 15g (39%)
Vitamin A (10.8%)
Calcium (14.8%)
Iron (10.4%)

pumpkin roll pancakes

10 MINS

20 MINS

30 MINS

I was craving a pumpkin roll today but making one of those was more of a project than I wanted to undertake. I decided to take the same flavors of pumpkin plus cream cheese icing and make pumpkin roll pancakes instead.

ingredients

BATTER INGREDIENTS:

- 4 eggs
- 1 cup cottage cheese
- 1 cup pumpkin puree
- 1/4 cup almond milk
- 1/3 cup almond flour
- 1/3 cup coconut flour
- 1/3 cup ground golden flax or additional almond flour
- 1 tsp vanilla
- 1 tsp baking powder
- 1/3 cup sugar free sweetener
- 1 tsp cinnamon
- 1/4 tsp ginger
- pinch of nutmeg

CREAM CHEESE ICING:

- 8 oz cream cheese softened
- 1/3 C sugar free sweetener

OR COTTAGE CHEESE ICING:

- 1 C cottage cheese
- 2 tbsp butter
- 1/4 C sugar free sweetener
- 1/2 tsp vanilla

directions

Combine all the ingredients in the blender putting the liquid ingredients in first. Blend until smooth.

Preheat a large frying pan over medium heat. Spray liberally with cooking spray. Drop Tbsps of dough onto the frying pan. I used a small cookie scoop for this. Cook well before flipping.

To make the cottage cheese icing: Blend cottage cheese until smooth in a small food processor or rocket blended. Add the other ingredients and mix well.

To make the cream cheese icing: Combine the cream cheese and sweetener and mix well.

Note: Larger pancakes may not cook through and may break when flipping.

nutrition facts

Amount Per Serving: 1/6

Calories 328

Total Fat 25.4g (39%)

Saturated Fat 13.6g (68%)

Cholesterol 154mg (51%)

Sodium 313mg (13%)

Total Carbohydrates 10.9g (4%)

Dietary Fiber 4.4g (18%)

Protein 14.9g

Vitamin A (141%)

Vitamin C (4%)

Calcium (14%)

Iron (2.5%)

Chapter Four

brunch sweets

When Sunday rolls around my family is longing for cinnamon rolls, donuts, coffee cakes, and danish. My brunch sweets are the perfect end to your morning. They go well with a cup of coffee and can double up for dessert when the day is over.

healthy gluten free cinnamon rolls

 30 MINS

40 MINS

1 HR 10 MINS

These healthy gluten free cinnamon rolls are perfect for lazy Sunday mornings. They have all the flavor without any sugar or grains. Low Carb, Keto, THM S.

ingredients

DOUGH INGREDIENTS:

- 8 oz shredded mozzerella (about 2 Cs)
- 2 oz cream cheese
- 1 egg
- 1/3 cup almond flour
- 1/3 cup coconut flour
- 1/3 cup ground golden flax (or additional almond flour)
- 2 tsp sugar free sweetener
- 1 tsp vanilla
- 1 tbsp baking powder

FILLING:

- 2 tbsp butter , softened
- 1/4 cup sugar free sweetener
- 1/2 tsp molasses (optional but this tiny amount adds negligible carbs and gives a nice flavor)
- 90 mg pure stevia extract, optional
- 2 tsp cinnamon

CREAM CHEESE ICING:

- 3 oz cream cheese , softened
- 1 tbsp butter , softened
- 1/4 C sugar free sweetener
- 1 tsp vanilla

directions

Preheat oven to 350.

Put cheese in a microwave-safe bowl. Microwave one minute. Stir. Microwave 30 seconds. Stir. At this point, all the cheese should be melted. Microwave 30 more seconds until uniform and gloopy (it should look like cheese fondue at this point).

Mix in the egg, vanilla, 2 tsp sweetener, baking powder, flours, and flax. Or pulse in a food processor until thoroughly combined. If mixing by hand you may need to dump it onto wax paper and knead it by hand to thoroughly incorporate the ingredients.

Once the dough is a uniform color wet your hands and press it out into a 9×12 ish rectangle on parchment paper.

Mix together the 1/4 C gentle sweet, stevia, cinnamon, and molasses (if using). Spread the dough with 2 tbsp of butter and sprinkle with sweetener combo. Roll up along the long side. Slice into 3/4 inch thick slices. Put them in a greased baking dish or pie plate.

Put the cinnamon buns into the oven. Bake for 35-40 min until golden brown.

Meanwhile, make the icing. Mix the cream cheese, butter, sweetener, and vanilla with an electric mixer until smooth. Set aside.

Let the cinnamon buns cool for 5 min and spread the icing over the top. Serve warm. You can reheat leftovers in the microwave.

nutrition facts

Amount Per Serving: 1
Calories 189
Calories from Fat 135
Total Fat 15g (23%)
Saturated Fat 7g (35%)
Cholesterol 49mg (16%)
Sodium 196mg (8%)
Potassium 178mg (5%)
Total Carbohydrates 5g (2%)
Dietary Fiber 3g (12%)
Protein 7g (14%)
Vitamin A (7.9%)
Calcium (17.5%)
Iron (4.3%)

pumpkin cinnamon rolls

 30 MINS

40 MINS

1HR 10 MINS

For an extra special brunch treat make these Pumpkin Cinnamon Rolls for your guests. They take the classic cream cheese covered cinnamon rolls and give them a fall twist that is delicious any time of the year.

ingredients

DONUTS:

- 1 cup mozzarella cheese
- 2 tbsp cream cheese
- 1 egg
- 2/3 cup almond flour
- 1/3 cup coconut flour
- 1 tbsp baking powder
- 1 tbsp sugar-free sweetener

FILLING:

- 1/4 cup pumpkin
- 1 tbsp butter
- 1 tsp vanilla
- 2 drops molasses, optional
- 3 tbsp sugar-free sweetener
- 2 tsp cinnamon
- 1/2 tsp nutmeg

ICING:

- 6 oz cream cheese
- 2 tbsp pumpkin puree
- 1/2 cup powdered erythritol

directions

Preheat oven to 350.

Put cheese in a microwave-safe bowl. Microwave one minute. Stir. Microwave 30 seconds. Stir. At this point, all the cheese should be melted. Microwave 30 more seconds until thoroughly melted (it should look like cheese fondue at this point).

Mix in the egg, flours, baking powder, and 1 tbsp sweetener by pulsing the dough ingredients in a food processor until thoroughly combined. If mixing by hand you may need to dump it onto wax paper and knead it by hand to thoroughly incorporate the ingredients.

Once the dough is a uniform color wet your hands and press it out into a 9×12 ish rectangle on parchment paper.

Mix together the pumpkin, butter, vanilla, and molasses. Spread the dough with the pumpkin filling and sprinkle with the sweetener, cinnamon, and nutmeg. Roll up along the long side. Slice into 3/4 inch thick slices. Put them in a greased baking dish or pie plate.

Put the cinnamon buns into the oven. Bake for 35-40 min until golden brown.

Meanwhile, make the icing. Mix the cream cheese, pumpkin puree, and sweetener with an electric mixer until smooth. Set aside.

Let the cinnamon buns cool for 5 min and spread the icing over the top. Serve warm. You can reheat leftovers in the microwave.

nutrition facts

Amount Per Serving: 1/12
Total Fat 11g (16%)
Saturated Fat 6g (29%)
Cholesterol 44mg (15%)
Sodium 157mg (7%)
Potassium 39mg (1%)
Total Carbohydrate 4g (1%)
Dietary Fiber 2g (6%)
Sugars 1g
Protein 4g (9%)
Vitamin A (16%)
Vitamin C (0%)
Calcium (8%)
Iron (4%)

glazed crumb donuts

30 MINS

35 MINS

1HR 5 MINS

A moist cakey donut topped with crumbs and covered with a sweet glaze. I wanted to make a copycat to the Entenmann's Glazed Crumb Donuts but didn't succeed. These are much better. I won't be tempted to grab one of those boxed assortments anymore.

ingredients

DONUTS:

- 2 tbsp butter softened
- 1/4 cup sour cream
- 2 tbsp sugar freesweetener
- 3 tbsp almond flour
- 3 tbsp coconut flour
- 2 tbsp ground golden flax or additional almond flour
- 1 egg
- 1 tsp vanilla
- 1/2 tsp baking powder
- tiny pinch of salt

CRUMB TOPPING:

- 1/2 C almond flour
- 2 tsp coconut flour
- 3 tbsp butter softened
- 3 tbsp sugar free sweetener

GLAZE:

- 2 tbsp butter
- 1/2 C sugar free sweetener

directions

Preheat the oven to 350.

Combine all the ingredients for the batter and mix well. Divide between twelve mini donut molds.

Combine the ingredients for the crumbs and mix well. They will be large moist crumbs. Spread them with your hands on top of the donut batter. You may need to break apart the large pieces into smaller crumbs.

Bake for 25 min. If the crumbs start to get too brown you can cover them with foil.

Meanwhile, make the glaze. In a small saucepan over low heat melt the butter and sweetener. Cook on low, whisking occasionally, for 12-15 minutes until golden. Cool for at least 10 minutes. Keep whisking occasionally as it cools to avoid it separating.

Cool the donuts and put them on a wire rack. Put a clean rimmed baking sheet under them. Spoon the glaze over the donuts. Then scoop up the glaze that dripped off onto the baking sheet and spoon it on them again. Repeat. This helps them get a nice thick coating. You will notice that the glaze keeps thickening.

nutrition facts

Amount Per Serving: 1

Calories 131

Calories from Fat 108

Total Fat 12g (18%)

Saturated Fat 5g (25%)

Cholesterol 33mg (11%)

Sodium 70mg (3%)

Potassium 32mg (1%)

Total Carbohydrates 2g (1%)

Dietary Fiber 1g (4%)

Protein 2g (4%)

Vitamin A (5.1%)

Calcium (3.7%)

Iron (2.5%)

braided blueberry cheese danish

 20 MINS

45 MINS

1 HR 5 MINS

This Braided Blueberry Cheese Danish has a golden brown dough, a ton of cream cheese filling, and blueberries that pop with every bite. It is a home run.

ingredients

DOUGH INGREDIENTS:

- 8 oz. shredded mozzarella about 2 cups
- 2 oz. cream cheese
- 1 egg
- 1/3 cup almond flour
- 1/3 cup coconut flour
- 1/3 cup ground golden flax or additional almond flour
- 1 tbsp sugar free sweetener
- 1 tsp vanilla

CREAM CHEESE FILLING:

- 8 oz. cream cheese softened
- 1 tsp vanilla
- 1 egg
- 1/4 C sugar free sweetener
- 3/4 C fresh or frozen blueberries do not thaw if using frozen

GLAZE (OPTIONAL):

- 1 tbsp softened butter
- 1 tbsp sugar free sweetener, finely ground
- 1/4 tsp vanilla

directions

Preheat the oven to 350.

Put cheese in a microwave-safe bowl. Microwave one minute. Stir. Microwave 30 seconds. Stir. At this point, all the cheese should be melted. Microwave 30 more seconds until uniform and gloopy (it should look like cheese fondue). Add the rest of the dough ingredients and the cheese to a food processor. Mix using the dough blade until a uniform color. If you do not have a food processor you can mix in a medium bowl with a wooden spoon. You may need to dump it onto wax paper and knead it by hand to thoroughly incorporate the ingredients. Once a uniform color, wet your hands and press it out into a 9×12 ish rectangle on a parchment-lined baking sheet.

To make the cream cheese filling you can add the cream cheese, vanilla, egg, and sweetener to the food processor (no need to wash) or to the bowl you were using. Mix until smooth in the food processor or with an electric mixer.

Put the filling down the center of the dough. Mine was spreading out a bit so I just pushed it back to the middle with a rubber spatula. Sprinkle the blueberries on top. Cut one-inch strips down the edges of the dough. Crisscross one over the other, braiding as you go down. Bake for 40-45 min until the dough is golden and the cheese filling no longer jiggles.

Optional glaze: Mix butter with of finely ground sweetener and vanilla. Put in a piping bag and drizzle over the top of the warm pastry (or just spread on top). It will melt and make a shiny glaze.

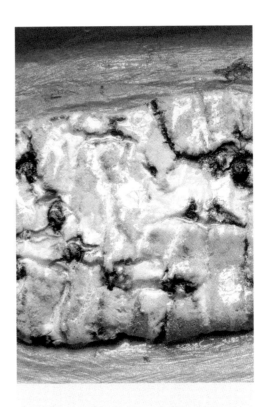

nutrition facts

Amount Per Serving: 1/12

Calories 211

Calories from Fat 153

Total Fat 17g (26%)

Saturated Fat 8g (40%)

Cholesterol 68mg (23%)

Sodium 213mg (9%)

Potassium 102mg (3%)

Total Carbohydrates 6g (2%)

Dietary Fiber 2g (8%)

Protein 8g (16%)

Vitamin A (9.8%)

Vitamin C (1.1%)

Calcium (14.1%)

Iron (4.4%)

cinnamon pecan crumb cake

15 MINS

40 MINS

55 MINS

Tender golden cake topped with a heaping pile of cinnamon pecan crumbs? Yes. My Cinnamon Crumb Cake Recipe is perfect for breakfast, brunch, dessert, or a mid-afternoon pick-me-up. That's my favorite time to cut a piece and savor every bite.

ingredients

CAKE:

- 1/2 cup almond flour
- 1/2 cup coconut flour
- 1/2 cup ground golden flax or additional almond flour
- 1/3 cup sugar free sweetener
- 4 eggs
- 4 oz half and half
- 2 oz cream cheese softened
- 2 tbsp butter softened
- 1 tsp vanilla extract
- 1 tsp cinnamon
- 1 tsp baking powder
- 1/4 tsp salt

TOPPING:

- 1 cup almond flour
- 1 cup pecans toasted
- 6 tbsp butter melted
- 1/3 cup sugar free sweetener
- 2 tsp cinnamon

directions

Preheat oven to 350.

Grease an 8×8 glass baking dish with butter or cooking spray.

In a bowl with an electric mixer combine all the batter ingredients. Mix thoroughly. Pour into the baking dish and spread evenly.

Combine topping ingredients in a food processor and pulse until crumbs form. Sprinkle on top of the batter.

Bake for 45-50 min until golden and the center feels firm to the touch. Do not underbake. If the topping starts to get too dark cover with foil for the last 10 minutes.

Store leftovers of this Cinnamon Pecan Crumb Cake in the refrigerator.

nutrition facts

Amount Per Serving: 1/16
Calories 236
Calories from Fat 189
Total Fat 21g (32%)
Saturated Fat 6g (30%)
Cholesterol 62mg (21%)
Sodium 126mg (5%)
Potassium 128mg (4%)
Total Carbohydrates 7g (2%)
Dietary Fiber 4g (16%)
Protein 6g (12%)
Vitamin A (6.3%)
Vitamin C (0.2%)
Calcium (7.7%)
Iron (6.8%)

Chapter Five

beverages

Joyful mornings in my home begin with a nice cup of coffee. As a mom of 5, I need that burst of caffeine to wake myself up. Even if you aren't a coffee drinker I have a variety of beverage recipes for you. If you prefer sweetened cream laden coffee, hot chocolate, creamy chai tea, or even a frozen vanilla frappe this chapter is for you.

sugar free hot chocolate mix

5 MINS

5 MINS

10 MINS

My Three Ingredient Instant Sugar Free Hot Chocolate Mix takes a family favorite and makes it healthier. With a batch of this on hand, even the kids can make their own sweet treat. THM S, Low Carb, Gluten Free, Dairy Free Option, Keto.

ingredients

- 1 cup sugar free sweetener
- 3/4 cup cocoa powder
- 3/4 cup heavy cream powder OR coconut milk powder

directions

Add the sweetener, cocoa, and heavy cream powder or coconut milk powder to a food processor and pulse to combine.

Mix 2 heaping Tbsps of hot chocolate mix into 10 oz very hot water. Stir to dissolve. Let cool for a few minutes before enjoying!

recipe notes

I've found that blending the powder helps it to dissolve better. I recommend taking the time for this extra step. You can double or triple my recipe to make a bigger batch.

nutrition facts

Amount Per Serving: 1/8
Calories 95
Calories from Fat 81
Total Fat 9g (14%)
Saturated Fat 5g (25%)
Cholesterol 30mg (10%)
Sodium 10mg (0%)
Potassium 184mg (4%)
Total Carbohydrates 5g (2%)
Dietary Fiber 2g (8%)
Protein 2g (4%)
Vitamin A (6.6%)
Vitamin C (0.2%)
Calcium (2.5%)
Iron (6.2%)

monkfruit coffee creamer

 5 MINS

0 MINS

5 MINS

This easy Monkfruit Coffee Creamer is perfect for both hot or iced coffee. You can easily adjust the sweetness to your taste buds and add extracts to customize.

ingredients

- 1 cup monkfruit erythritol blend sweetener, such as Lakanto
- 1/2 cup water
- 1/2 tsp vanilla
- 1 1/2 cups almond milk
- 1 1/2 cups heavy cream

directions

Combine sweetener and water in a small saucepan and heat on medium just until the sweetener melts.

Cool to room temperature and mix in the other ingredients. Store in the fridge.

nutrition facts

Amount Per Serving: 1/4
Calories 83
Total Fat 9g (13%)
Saturated Fat 5g (26%)
Cholesterol 31mg (10%)
Sodium 42mg (2%)
Total Carbohydrates 1g (0%)
Protein 1g (4%)
Vitamin A (8%)
Vitamin C (0%)
Calcium (7%)
Iron (1%)

sugar free starbucks vanilla latte frappuccino

 5 MINS

0 MINS

5 MINS

If you've been missing a good vanilla iced latte or frappuccino you've come to the right place. Make one concentrate and have your favorite beverage ready in minutes. It is even faster than waiting on line to order one.

ingredients

- 1 1/2 cups almond milk
- 1/2 cup heavy cream
- 1 cup very very strong coffee (I used twice the amount of grounds I normally use)
- 1/2 cup sugar free sweetener
- 1 tsp vanilla

directions

Combine concentrate ingredients and mix thoroughly.

VARIATIONS:

Iced Latte: 1 part concentrate, 1 to 1.5 parts almond milk, to taste, coffee ice cubes (highly recommended - just freeze coffee in an ice cube tray)

Latte Example: 6 oz concentrate plus 8 oz of almond milk over a few frozen coffee ice cubes

Frappuccino: Blend 1 part concentrate, 1/2 part almond milk, coffee ice cubes and regular ice cubes, and a pinch of xanthan gum, optional (it helps keep the drink from separating)

Frappuccino Example: 8 oz concentrate plus 4 oz almond milk blended with 6 coffee ice cubes, 6 regular ice cubes, and a pinch of xanthan gum

recipe notes

Store in the fridge for up to a week to quickly make
your favorite beverage.

nutrition facts

Amount Per Serving: 4 oz.

Total Fat 8g (12%)

Saturated Fat 4g (20%)

Cholesterol 27mg (9%)

Sodium 89mg (4%)

Potassium 34mg (1%)

Vitamin A (5.8%)

Calcium (8.8%)

instant chai tea mix

5 MINS

0 MINS

5 MINS

I love sweet, creamy, hot chai tea on a cold day. One year I even made instant chai tea mix and gave it as a gift to friends and relatives. It had powdered milk, powdered creamer, sugar, instant tea powder, and all the chai spices. I decided to give that recipe a makeover.

ingredients

- 1/2 cup sugar free sweetener
- 1/2 cup heavy cream powder or coconut milk powder
- 2 tsp cinnamon
- 1 tsp ground ginger
- 1/4 tsp each ground allspice, cardamon, cloves, nutmeg*

directions

Whisk together all the ingredients.

To serve: Pour 12 oz boiling water over 2 tea bags. Let steep until the desired strength is obtained. Stir in 3-4 tbsp instant chai tea mix. Add a few drops of vanilla if desired. Sip and smile.

VARIATIONS:

To make this a fuel pull just leave out the heavy cream powder and add almond milk after you add the mix. Start with 1 tbsp of the mix and taste.

To make this dairy free just leave out the heavy cream powder and add a splash of coconut milk after you add the mix. Start with 1 tbsp of the mix and taste.

recipe notes

*Some of these are pricey and I don't use them very often. My recommendation is to buy whole spices and then grind them as needed. They can last years that way. These measurements will make 4–5 Cs of chai tea. You can make this in larger quantities if desired.

nutrition facts

Amount Per Serving: 4

Calories 107

Calories from Fat 99

Total Fat 11g (17%)

Saturated Fat 6g (30%)

Cholesterol 40mg (13%)

Sodium 11mg (0%)

Potassium 22mg (1%)

Total Carbohydrates 2g (1%)

Vitamin A (8.7%)

Calcium (3.2%)

Iron (1.1%)

Made in the USA
Columbia, SC
27 December 2019